Our Senses

SMELL

Kay Woodward

GARETH **STEVENS**

GS

PUBLISHING

A World Almanac Education Group Company

Please visit our web site at: www.garethstevens.com
For a free color catalog describing Gareth Stevens Publishing's
list of high-quality books and multimedia programs, call
1-800-542-2595 (USA) or 1-800-387-3178 (Canada).
Gareth Stevens Publishing's fax: (414) 332-3567.

Library of Congress Cataloging-in-Publication Data

Woodward, Kay.
    Smell / Kay Woodward.
        p. cm — (Our senses)
    Includes index.
    ISBN 0-8368-4408-4 (lib. bdg.)
    1. Smell—Juvenile literature. I. Title.
QP458.W65   2005
612.8'6—dc22   2004052570

This North American edition first published in 2005 by
Gareth Stevens Publishing
A World Almanac Education Group Company
330 West Olive Street, Suite 100
Milwaukee, Wisconsin 53212 USA

This U.S. edition copyright © 2005 by Gareth Stevens, Inc.
Original edition copyright © 2005 by Hodder Wayland.
First published in 2005 by Hodder Wayland, an imprint of
Hodder Children's Books, a division of Hodder Headline
Limited, 338 Euston Road, London NW1 3BH, U.K.

Commissioning Editor: Victoria Brooker
Book Editor: Katie Sergeant
Consultant: Carol Ballard
Picture Research: Katie Sergeant
Book Designer: Jane Hawkins
Cover: Hodder Children's Books

Gareth Stevens Editor: Barbara Kiely Miller
Gareth Stevens Designer: Kami Koenig

Printed in China

1 2 3 4 5 6 7 8 9 09 08 07 06 05

Picture Credits
Alamy: 9 (Christa Knijff/Royalty-Free); Corbis: imprint page, 18
(Philippe Eranian), 4 (Norbert Schaefer), 5 (O'Brien Productions/
Kevin Cozad), 7 (James Leynse), 8 (Saba/Najlah Feanny), 12
(Sygma/Baumgartner Olivia), 13 (Walter Hodges), 15 (Massimo
Mastrorillo), 17 (Paul A. Souders), 19 (Kennan Ward); Getty
Images: cover (Taxi/Dana Edmunds), 10 (White Packert), 14
(Photographer's Choice), 20 (The Image Bank/Luis Castaneda, Inc.),
21 (Stone/Rosemary Calvert); Shout: 16 (John Callan); Wayland
Picture Library: title page, 11, 22, 23 (both). The artwork on page
6 is by Peter Bull.

About the Author
Kay Woodward is an experienced children's author who
has written over twenty nonfiction and fiction titles.

About the Consultant
Carol Ballard is an elementary school science
coordinator. She is the author of many books for
children and is a consultant for several publishers.

CONTENTS

Words in **bold** type can be found in the glossary.

SMELLS ALL AROUND!

The world is filled with many **smells**, or **scents**. Different objects have different smells. Flowers and freshly baked bread and cookies smell nice. Rotten eggs and garbage smell nasty.

Our **sense** of smell makes us able to take in all the amazing smells around us. We use our noses to smell. We also use our noses to breathe. Air and smells enter the nose through holes called **nostrils**.

HOW YOUR NOSE WORKS

Smells travel through the air and into your nose. Information about the smells is then sent to your brain, which **identifies** them. This is how you smell things.

This is what a nose looks like from the inside.

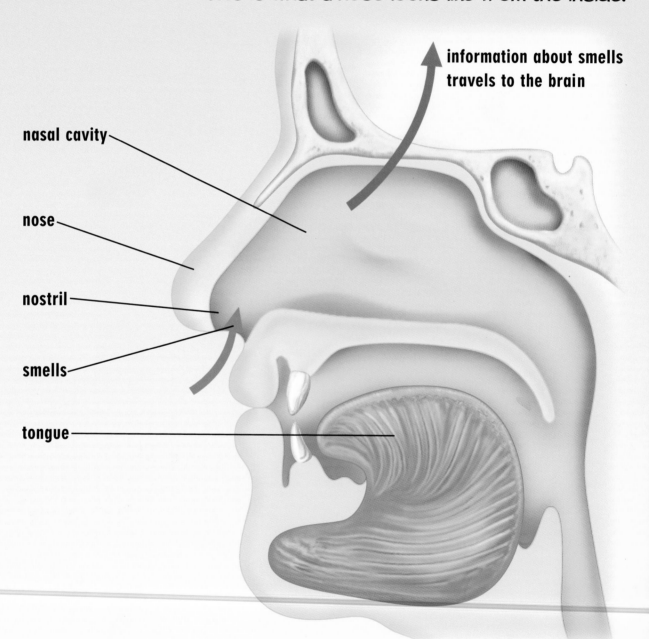

information about smells travels to the brain

nasal cavity

nose

nostril

smells

tongue

You can smell an object better by **sniffing** deeply. The closer you are to the object, the stronger its smell will be.

NICE SMELLS

Most foods smell so delicious that they make you want to eat. Pizza, popcorn, and oranges smell good. Chili smells spicy. Hot chocolate smells sweet.

There are many amazing smells outdoors. Trees, plants, and flowers have beautiful scents. The ocean smells salty. Fresh air smells crisp and clean.

DIFFERENT SMELLS

Everybody is different, and we each have our own sense of smell. We like the smells of some things, but we do not like the smells of others.

Not everybody likes the smell of fish.

Some people might like to smell strawberries.
Other people might like to smell onions.
What do you like to smell?

SMELLING CLEARLY

When you have a cold, your nose usually gets stuffed up, and you may not be able to smell properly.

Also, as people get older, they often find it harder to recognize smells.

Some people cannot smell at all. They may have lost their sense of smell because of an injury or illness. People without a sense of smell find it difficult to taste foods.

Our senses of smell and taste work together.

NASTY SMELLS

Our sense of smell sometimes tells us when foods are **spoiled**. Moldy food smells bad. Old milk smells sour. When foods smell bad, we should not eat or drink them.

Cars pump smelly dirt and smoke out of their exhaust pipes. In cities with busy streets, the air can get very dirty. When air is dirty, we say it is **polluted**.

In the busy city of Bangkok, in Thailand, the air is very polluted.

DANGER!

Gas has a strong smell.

Some smells warn us of danger. A **gas** leak could cause a huge **explosion**. If you ever smell gas, you should immediately tell an adult.

Where there is fire, there is always smoke. Anytime you smell smoke, you should tell an adult or dial 911 to call the fire department. You might save someone's life.

Fire is extremely dangerous.

ANIMALS AND SMELL

A dog has an amazing sense of smell. Dogs can smell many things that people cannot smell. Some dogs are specially trained to use their sense of smell to find and rescue people in the snow.

Bears use their sense of smell to find food. Polar bears have a sense of smell that is one hundred times better than ours. They can smell seals that are more than 20 miles (32 kilometers) away.

INSECTS AND SMELL

Most insects use their antennae to smell. An insect's antennae are the two long, thin body parts that stick out of its head.

Insects send information to each other using different smells. They give off one kind of smell when they are looking for a **mate**. They give off another kind when they are looking for food.

Ladybugs smell through their antennae to find the small insects they like to eat.

WHAT DO YOU SMELL?

Find out how good your sense of smell is with this simple experiment. Ask your friends to join in. Make sure you have an adult to help you.

1. Gather lots of different "smelly" foods and objects. Here are some ideas:

   oranges
   ground coffee or coffee beans
   onions
   chocolate
   soap
   cheese
   scented candles

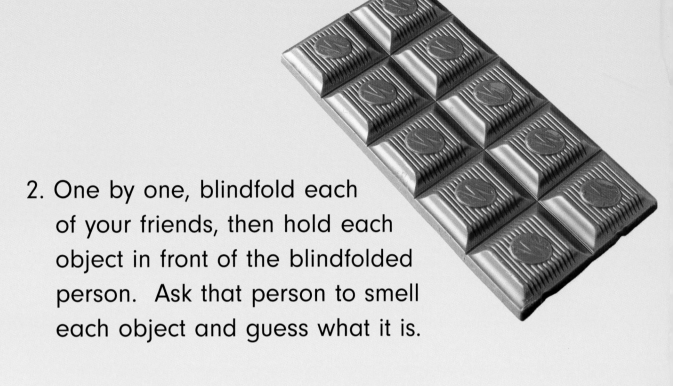

2. One by one, blindfold each of your friends, then hold each object in front of the blindfolded person. Ask that person to smell each object and guess what it is.

3. Now you try to guess the smells.

4. How many did you get right? Were any smells easier to guess than others?

GLOSSARY

explosion: the act of bursting apart with great force, noise, and heat

gas: an invisible, airlike substance. We burn natural gas for fuel.

identifies: recognizes something as being a certain object or person

mate: one of a pair of animals that, together, can produce young

nostrils: holes at the bottom of the nose, through which air and smells enter the body

polluted: unclean or impure, made dirty by the addition of smoke, harmful chemicals, or man-made waste

scents: particular smells, or odors

sense: a natural ability to receive and process information using one or more of the body's sense organs, such as the ears, eyes, nose, tongue, or skin. The five senses are hearing, sight, smell, taste, and touch.

smell: (n) the scent, or odor, of something; the sense used to receive and identify odors; (v) to breathe in through the nose and recognize different scents, or odors

sniffing: taking strong, quick breaths through the nose

spoiled: not fit for use because it is too old or has rotted

INDEX